Hannigan, Lynne
    Harvest festival.–(Celebrations series)
    1. Harvest festivals–Juvenile literature
    I. Title   II. Nagrath, Renu   III. Series
    394.2'683   GT4380

    ISBN 0–7136–2935–5

For our parents

Published by A&C Black (Publishers) Ltd
35 Bedford Row
London WC1R 4JH

Acknowledgements
The authors and publisher would like to thank the teachers and pupils
of Manor Infants School, Reverend Brian Goss, Kellie and her family,
and Mr Estelle at the allotment.

Filmset by August Filmsetting, Haydock, St Helens
Printed in Portugal by Resopal Lda

Harvest Festival

Lynne Hannigan and Renu Nagrath

Photographs by Ed Barber

A&C Black · London

Hello, my name is Kellie.

I've brought this box of food for our Harvest Festival at school. Everyone is bringing some food to share. We're going to have a special assembly to say thank you for all the good things which we have to eat.

There's already lots of food in the hall — fruit and vegetables, tea and even a tin of biscuits.

2

My Auntie Betty has given us some potatoes. She grew them herself.

Near where she lives, there's a big piece of ground which is divided into lots of little gardens called allotments. Auntie Betty grows vegetables and flowers on her allotment.

Our teacher, Miss Nagrath, is taking us to the allotments so we can see some of the vegetables which are ready to eat at harvest time. We're going by mini-bus.

Shirley, the driver, helps us down from the bus.

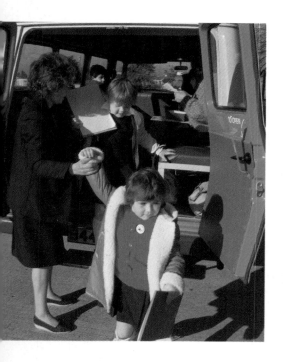

Then we have to jump over some big puddles. I'm glad I've got my boots on.

4

Auntie Betty and Mr Estelle are waiting for us.
Mr Estelle is in charge of the allotments. He tells
us that harvest time in the countryside is when
farmers cut down the wheat in their fields.
Mr Estelle doesn't grow wheat on the allotments,
but we can pick some flowers instead.

Mr Estelle lets us have a look in the tool shed, and Melanie tries out the big fork.

Then Auntie Betty digs up some potatoes for us.

We help to dig up some carrots, too. They look
very dirty, but Niss Nagrath says it's only earth.
She says that plants need food, just like we do,
and they get some of their food from the earth.

'Look at these cabbages!' says Stephen.
Some of the cabbages are nearly as tall as us.

Some are just
beginning to
grow.

8

Sajida finds some Chinese onions. She's trying to get a closer look but she doesn't want to get her shoes dirty.

On the way back, we pass a big pile of old leaves. It smells funny. Miss Nagrath says it's a compost heap. The leaves will go soft and rotten. Then they can be spread on the earth to help the plants grow.

We're going to paint all the things we saw at the allotments. I'm painting the vegetables.

We try to think of some different places where people grow things.

'My dad grows tomatoes in a grow-bag,' says Ryan.

'My mum grows herbs in our garden,' says Jagdev.

An allotment at Harvest time.

We visited an allotment.

We saw ....

raspberries, marrow, runner beans, brussel sprouts, potatoes, and carrots.

store huts

We got some beans to grow from the farm shop.

We dug some potatoes from the ground.

some huge cabbages,

Green tomatos ripen in the sun and turn red.

A store-hou to keep ha

chrysanthemums,

beetroot,

compost heap

a fork

a hoe

a bucket

a cat

water tank

We put Auntie Betty and Mr Estelle in our painting.
There's water and compost for the vegetables.
We put the sun in the picture, too, because plants
need sunlight to make them grow.

Today, there's a market near our school. We're having a look at the fruit and vegetable stalls.

We saw some of these vegetables at the allotments.

'What's this?' says Daniel. Miss Nagrath says it's a pomegranate. She's going to buy some different kinds of fruit so everyone can have a taste.

Some of the fruit in the market comes from countries a long way away. We look at the empty boxes to see where the fruit came from.

We are looking at
pineapples when
Miss Nagrath sees her
mum. She is buying a
box of papaya. The box is
very heavy, so we decide
to take it home in the
mini-bus for her.

Some of the others stop to watch a busker in the market. He is playing the saxophone and collecting money in his hat. They watch him for ages, and they are almost late back for the bus.

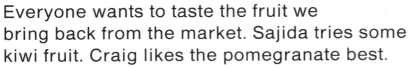
avocado pear

Everyone wants to taste the fruit we
bring back from the market. Sajida tries some
kiwi fruit. Craig likes the pomegranate best.

Miss Nagrath says that these fruits grow
in hot countries and are sent to Britain
by ship.

They
our

People buy big quantities
and sell them in smaller
quantities.

They get ●●●●●
from our 10p.

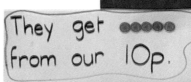

Yy   Zz

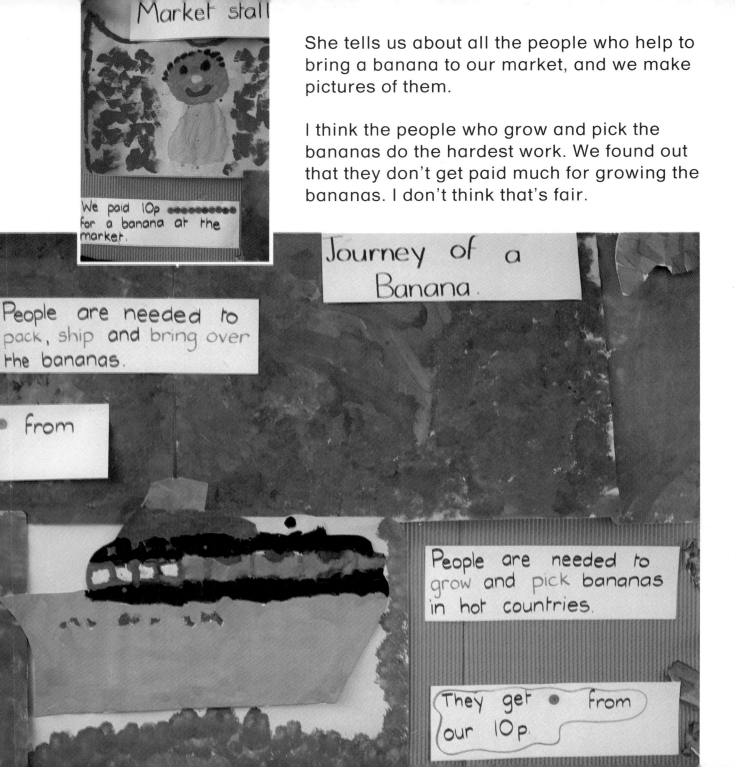

Market stall

We paid 10p ●●●●●●●●●● for a banana at the market.

She tells us about all the people who help to bring a banana to our market, and we make pictures of them.

I think the people who grow and pick the bananas do the hardest work. We found out that they don't get paid much for growing the bananas. I don't think that's fair.

Journey of a Banana.

People are needed to pack, ship and bring over the bananas.

● from

People are needed to grow and pick bananas in hot countries.

They get ● from our 10p.

On Sunday, Mum and I go to church. Our Minister is Reverend Goss. He's pleased because we've brought a box of fruit for the church Harvest Festival.

In church, we say prayers and sing hymns to thank God for our food.

Afterwards, I ask Reverend Goss if he knows about the story of the banana which we heard at school.

At school today, we're making some bread for harvest. We mix up flour and salt and water with some yeast to make the dough.

I'm doing the hard work, pushing and pulling the dough. It's called 'kneading' but you do it with your hands, not your knees.

We make the dough into rolls and cook them in the oven. They smell lovely!

Miss Nagrath and Raheela's mum have brought some different kinds of bread to show us. There's a round flat bread called a roti and a special harvest loaf with a little mouse on it.

We are ready for our harvest assembly. Look at all the flowers and food we've brought!

Reverend Brownut comes to talk to us in assembly. He says harvest is a good time to think about sharing and giving. After assembly we give the food and flowers to some old people who have come to see us.

We're having bread and soup today instead of school dinner. Then we can share our dinner money with people who don't get enough to eat.

23

It's nearly home time and I'm thinking about our assembly. I'm thinking about Auntie Betty, too. When I get home, I'm going to give her a big hug because she is good at sharing.

More about Harvest Festival

Every day of the year, people are harvesting crops somewhere in the world, and many different countries celebrate harvest in their own way. In Britain, most crops ripen between June and September, so we celebrate harvest at the end of our summer.

Until a few hundred years ago, many ordinary people in Britain had to grow their own food. It was difficult and expensive to transport food for long distances, so a bad harvest meant that people would go hungry.

Nowadays, food can be treated so that it lasts a long time and can be shipped over great distances. Most people in Britain buy their food from shops and don't go hungry because of a bad harvest. But Christians in Britain still celebrate Harvest Festival in churches and schools.

People bring garden produce, wheat, bread or other gifts to the harvest service. They say prayers and sing hymns to thank God for their food. Now that so much of our food comes from other countries, harvest is also a time to think of the people all over the world who help to grow our food and bring it to us, and who are sometimes not so well off as we are.

Things to do

1. Lots of things we eat every day are made from grain. There are different kinds of grain: rice, wheat, barley, corn and maize. Look in your kitchen cupboard and see if any of your breakfast cereals have those words written on them. Do you eat corn flakes or puffed wheat?

What can you cook with your different kinds of grain? Bread, roti, rice and peas, rice pudding, popcorn or porridge. Can you think of any more?

2. Perhaps you can grow something for yourself. On a piece of wet blotting paper in a jar, you could grow cress or mung beans. Try growing herbs, or you could grow tomatoes in a grow-bag.

3. You can play a word game. How many words can you make from the word 'Harvest'? Here are two to help you start – 'share', 'save'.

4. Look at the harvest in the place where you live. It may not be food, it may be cars or glass. Factories give us a harvest of different things we need.

5. Have you heard of a harvest mouse? Find out about one in your library. Draw a picture and write about it.

6. At harvest time, people thank God in many different ways. Jewish people celebrate Succoth and the Japanese have a New Taste festival. Find out what you can about these and other harvest festivals.

7. Find out if there is an allotment or farm you can visit.

8. Make a calendar about something you can watch growing. Note down the weather, and the crop's progress each month until it is fully grown.

9. Collect labels and the empty packaging from the food in your supermarket trolley. Find out where the food comes from.

Books for you to read

Harvest and Thanksgiving, *by Ralph Whitlock* (Wayland)
The Farmer, *by Anne Stewart,* (Hamish Hamilton)
A Farming Family from Wales, *by Robin Gwyndaf,* (A & C Black)
One World on your Doorstep. Planner's handbook for One World Week and other events, *by Maggie Murray,* (Christian Aid). Christian Aid has books and posters as well as other information about sharing. Its address is Christian Aid, P.O. Box No. 1, London SW9 8BH.